SOCIAL STUDIES EXPLORER

It's Cool to Learn About America's Waterways

THE COLORADO RIVER

◆→ by Katie Marsico

CHERRY LAKE PUBLISHING • ANN ARBOR, MICHIGAN

Published in the United States of America
by Cherry Lake Publishing
Ann Arbor, Michigan
www.cherrylakepublishing.com

Content Adviser: James Wolfinger, PhD, Associate Professor,
History and Teacher Education, DePaul University, Chicago, Illinois

Book Design: The Design Lab

Photo Credits: Cover and page 3, ©Sally Scott/Shutterstock, Inc., ©Andy
Z./Shutterstock, Inc., ©Sydneymills/Shutterstock, Inc., ©Robert Fullerton/
Shutterstock, Inc., ©Boris15/Shutterstock, Inc.; Back cover and page 3,
©iStockphoto.com/skibreck; page 5, ©Kevin Ebi/Alamy; page 6, ©iofoto/
Shutterstock, Inc.; page 8, ©Barbara Helgason/Dreamstime.com; page 9,
©Chris Curtis/Shutterstock, Inc.; page 10, ©Bluerabbi/Dreamstime.com;
page 11, ©Jim Feliciano/Shutterstock, Inc.; page 12, ©Vicki Smith/Alamy;
page 13, ©Ron Niebrugge/Alamy; page 15, ©Tom Reichner/Shutterstock,
Inc.; page 16, ©Matt Jeppson/Shutterstock, Inc.; page 18, ©Pictorial
Press Ltd/Alamy; page 19, ©Timrobertsaeria/Dreamstime.com; page 21,
©Cafebeanz Company/Dreamstime.com; page 22, ©John Elk III/Alamy;
page 23, ©tacar/Shutterstock, Inc.; page 26, ©Zainkapas/Dreamstime.
com; page 28, ©Thaerjoseph/Dreamstime.com.

Library of Congress Cataloging-in-Publication Data
Marsico, Katie, 1980–
    The Colorado River / by Katie Marsico.
        p. cm. — (It's cool to learn about America's waterways)
(Explorer library)
    Includes bibliographical references and index.
    ISBN 978-1-62431-014-0 (lib. bdg.) — ISBN 978-1-62431-038-6 (pbk.)
— ISBN 978-1-62431-062-1 (e-book)
1. Colorado River (Colo.-Mexico)—Juvenile literature. 2. Colorado River
(Colo.-Mexico)—Geography—Juvenile literature. I. Title.
    F788.M375 2013
    979.1'3—dc23   2012036043

Cherry Lake Publishing would like to acknowledge the work
of The Partnership for 21st Century Skills. Please visit
www.21stcenturyskills.org for more information.

Printed in the United States of America
Corporate Graphics Inc.
January 2013
CLSP12

THE COLORADO RIVER

TABLE OF CONTENTS

JOHN WESLEY POWELL

6c U.S. POSTAGE

1869 EXPEDITION

CHAPTER ONE

WELCOME TO THE COLORADO RIVER!

➻ Thrill seekers from around the country travel to the Colorado River for the excitement of white-water rafting.

Are you excited about exploring the Colorado River? Americans have nicknamed this waterway the Lifeline of the Southwest! (A lifeline is something that people depend on to survive.) During your journey, you'll spot desert tortoises, black bears, and small, spiny trees called mesquites. You'll also tour parts of the Grand Canyon and experience the thrill of **white-water** rafting. Along the way, you'll learn about local Native American culture. You'll also get a chance to sample Southwestern **cuisine**. Most importantly, you'll discover what simple steps you can take to care for the Colorado River.

Before you begin your adventure, you need to find out exactly where you're headed. The Colorado River starts in northern Colorado's Rocky Mountains and runs for roughly 1,500 miles (2,414 kilometers). It flows southwest until it reaches the area around the Arizona–Nevada border. The river then curves south toward the Sea of Cortez, also known as the Gulf of California.

The Colorado River's watershed measures approximately 240,000 square miles (621,597 square kilometers). A watershed, or basin, is the region drained by a river and all of its **tributaries**. The Colorado River's upper basin includes parts of Wyoming, Utah, Colorado, and New Mexico. Its lower basin reaches across California, Arizona, and Nevada.

Hurry! Grab a pencil and jot down a few fast facts. Let's look at the portion of the Colorado River that flows through the Grand Canyon. The average depth of this section of the waterway is 40 feet (12 meters), and the average width is 300 feet (91 m). Be aware, though, that this only describes 280 miles (451 km) of the Colorado River. Measurements may be different in other areas.

➥ Water from the Colorado River helps keep nearby farmland fertile, or capable of producing crops.

Are you wondering what exactly makes the Colorado River the Lifeline of the Southwest? The answer is that it provides water to roughly 35 million people. The river is also used to **irrigate** about 3.5 million acres (1.4 million hectares) of farmland. Experts say that more water is taken out of the Colorado River basin than any other river basin in the world.

You may have already guessed that exploring one of the most important rivers in the Southwest will keep you quite busy. Of course, you don't want to tire yourself out. So, for your first tour of the Colorado River, you should probably limit your journey to the United States. You can always check out Mexico during your second adventure along the waterway!

ACTIVITY

COLORADO RIVER MAP

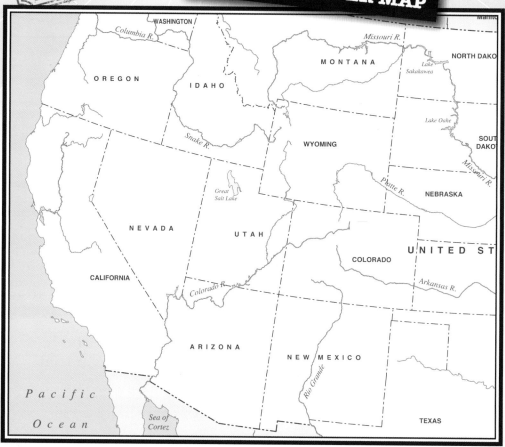

Take a few minutes to study this map of the Colorado River.
Then lay a separate piece of paper over it and trace the
waterway's outline. Label the Sea of Cortez. Do the same
for the upper and lower basins, as well as Wyoming, Utah,
Colorado, New Mexico, California, Arizona, Nevada, and Mexico.
Feel free to add any other important locations you read
about as you continue exploring the Colorado River!

STOP
Don't write in
this book!

●◆ The Colorado River begins in the Rocky Mountains.

Just because you're visiting a river doesn't mean that you will be spending all of your time in the water! The Colorado River's **ecosystem** includes an extremely wide variety of natural **habitats**. You'll explore a snowy mountain environment near the waterway's source high up in the Rockies. From 12,000 feet (3,658 m) above sea level, the river tumbles downward and across portions of Colorado and Utah. These areas are shaped by colorful cliffs and canyons. Small pine and juniper trees make up the desert woodlands, or forests, that cover the region.

The Colorado River next twists southwest toward Arizona and carves out the Grand Canyon. Here, you will travel through thick forests of trees and shrubs that grow along

the waterway. As you journey westward into Nevada, you'll have a chance to study habitats in the Mojave Desert. This section of the lower basin is famous for its hot, dry, and often harsh environment. Yet you'll also find unique **springs** and man-made lakes not far from where the Colorado River flows through the desert.

Farther south, the river winds along the Arizona–California border toward Mexico and the Sea of Cortez. You'll get a peek at the Sonoran Desert in this part of the lower basin. There are also several marshes and **backwaters**. Unfortunately, by the end of your trip, you'll discover how human activity has destroyed many of the natural wetlands that used to exist there. For now, though, turn your attention to local weather so you can decide what to put in your suitcase!

Cactuses dot the landscape in the Sonoran Desert.

Should you pack a heavy winter jacket or a tank top and shorts for your adventure? A lot depends on when and where you will be traveling. Be sure you have gloves and a scarf if you plan to be near the source, or headwaters, of the Colorado River in winter. In January, temperatures often dip as low as 16 degrees Fahrenheit (−8.9 degrees Celsius) in this portion of the Rockies. Do you have a pair of boots? In March, you might see as much as 8.6 inches (21.8 centimeters) of snow there! The climate close to the river's headwaters tends to be cold and humid. However, it is generally arid throughout the rest of the upper and lower basins. In other words, it is extremely dry, with little to no rainfall.

•❖ During winter, ice sometimes forms on parts of the Colorado River.

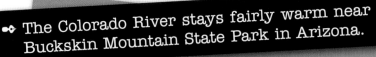

•o The Colorado River stays fairly warm near Buckskin Mountain State Park in Arizona.

If you head to where the river runs through the Mojave Desert, you'll find that summer temperatures climb higher than 110°F (43.3°C). It's not unusual for that area to receive less than 5 inches (13 cm) of rain each year.

What about a bathing suit? Water temperatures in the Colorado River are also affected by the season and your location. In the waters that flow through Buckskin Mountain State Park in western Arizona, readings range from 52°F (11.1°C) to 77°F (25.0°C). Prepare for slightly chillier conditions in the upper basin. For instance, year-round water temperatures in Glen Canyon in southern Utah stay at about 46°F (7.8°C). Keep the local climate in mind as you continue packing. You still have to gather a few other items if you truly want to be ready to tour the Colorado River.

CHAPTER TWO

THE WATERWAY'S WILDLIFE

➤ Pinyons are generally shorter than other types of pines.

Do you own a journal or notebook? Be sure to pack it, along with a pen or pencil. These will help you describe the amazing wildlife that lives in and along the Colorado River. You should record everything you see, hear, and smell as you look for local species.

For starters, breathe in deeply when you visit the upper basin. If you like the scent of Christmas trees, you'll enjoy taking a whiff of low-growing pine trees called pinyons. While you're traveling through the Rockies, you'll also spot junipers,

spruces, firs, aspens, and a variety of shrubs such as sage-brush. As the Colorado River flows south, you'll be able to relax in the shade of cottonwood, water birch, and box elder trees. Wildflowers bloom near the river, too. Bring a camera to snap photos of columbines, daisies, buttercups, and forget-me-nots. These are found throughout the upper basin.

At the Grand Canyon, keep your eyes peeled for coyote willow. Look for evergreen shrubs called arrowweed and western honey mesquites, too. Later, when you arrive in the Mojave Desert, be on the lookout for beavertail and cholla cactuses. Despite the dryness and heat, colorful desert primroses and sunflowers also grow there. As the river rushes toward the U.S. border, local marshes provide a habitat for reedlike plants known as bulrushes.

◦◦ A surprising variety of shrubs, flowers, and grasses line the Colorado River as it passes through the Mojave Desert.

Binoculars are always a help when exploring. They let you take a closer peek at the animals living in and around the Colorado River. You might study the black bears, bighorn sheep, elk, and snowshoe hares that are found in the upper basin. There's a good chance you'll also see beavers, coyotes, mountain lions, and mule deer. Marmots—which are basically large ground squirrels—also live in this region.

Aim your binoculars toward the sky as well! Birds such as American dippers, Canada geese, and ospreys fly over the upper basin. Great blue herons, bald eagles, and peregrine falcons are also common. In addition, this area is home to several types of **amphibians** and reptiles. These include tiger salamanders,

Much of the wildlife living in or along the Colorado River depends on a freshwater environment to survive. Closer to the Sea of Cortez, certain animals such as the vaquita porpoise and large fish called totoabas exist in brackish water. Brackish water is a combination of freshwater and salty seawater.

➡ Male mule deer grow pointed antlers that they often use to fight one another.

western toads, milk snakes, and large lizards called chuckwallas. Don't forget that the river's ecosystem also has many different kinds of fish. Cutthroat trout, humpback chubs, and mountain suckers are just a few species that swim through the waterway's upper section.

You'll need to cover a lot more ground—and water— to observe all of the river's wildlife. Certain animals such as bighorn sheep, mountain lions, and mule deer exist in both basins. The lower basin is also a habitat for river otters and bats.

➥ A desert tortoise relies upon its hard shell for protection from enemies.

Be ready to do some serious bird-watching in the lower basin! Burrowing owls, mallards, hummingbirds, rock wrens, California condors, and northern goshawks are all members of the Colorado River ecosystem. Local reptiles include rattle-snakes, desert tortoises, and lizards called Gila monsters. You might glimpse amphibians such as canyon tree frogs and red-spotted toads in the lower basin, as well.

If you're lucky, you'll get a look at one of the Colorado River's most famous fish—the razorback sucker. Razorbacks often grow longer than 3 feet (0.9 m) and weigh up to 13 pounds (5.9 kilograms). Some live more than 40 years. Unfortunately, this species is endangered. This means it is at risk of being completely wiped off the planet. Soon you'll learn more about what you can do to help save animals such as the razorback sucker. In the meantime, zip your suitcase and start moving. You're about to officially begin your adventure along a remarkable American waterway!

Make Your Very Own Field Guide

Are you a bit worried about how to keep track of the countless plants and animals that live in and along the Colorado River? You'll be off to a great start if you use a field guide! You might own a field guide that focuses on the Colorado River. If not, you can easily create your own! First, pick 20 local species (or more if you want). Write the name of each one on a separate sheet of paper. Then get ready to do some detective work on the computer or at the library. Track down and record the following information for the plants and animals you have selected:

Type of plant/animal: (tree, shrub, flower/reptile, mammal, fish)
Habitat:
Appearance:
Other interesting facts:

After you're done, you can either print out or sketch pictures of the species in your field guide. Finally, decorate a cover and staple your pages together. You can also snap them into a binder. Be sure to have your field guide handy when you arrive at the Colorado River!

CHAPTER THREE

PAST AND PRESENT

→ The Apaches were among the first people to settle in the area surrounding the Colorado River.

You're so close to the Colorado River that you can almost hear the sound of rushing water. Hang on for just a few more minutes, though. You need to go on a little side trip. Prepare to briefly travel through time to explore the history of this U.S. waterway!

Volcanic eruptions and the movement of plates, or pieces, of the earth's surface shaped the area that now makes up the Colorado River basin. This activity happened tens of millions of years ago! Believe it or not, the Colorado River used to mainly flow west. Today, it flows southwest. About 5 million years ago, land shifted, mountains rose, and the river started to run in its present direction.

Now jump ahead in your journey through time. Roughly 12,000 years ago, early peoples began living in the Colorado River watershed. In the centuries that followed, several Native American groups developed villages throughout the upper and lower basins. They included the Apache, Cocopah, Goshute, Halchidhoma, Havasupai, Hopi, Hualapai, Jano, Jocome, Maricopa, Mojave, Navajo, O'odham, Paiute, Pueblo, Shoshone, Sumo, Ute, Yavapai, Yuma, and Zuni.

During the 16th century, Europeans began exploring the Colorado River. The United States gained control over most of the watershed in the 1800s. Beginning in the late 1800s, Americans constructed dams and canals along the river. People relied on the river to support the Southwest's **economy**. Today, tourism, **recreational** activities, and farming are all important businesses in the Colorado River basin.

Do you think you might want to have a home in the Colorado River basin someday? Perhaps you already do! Either way, experts suspect that the watershed's population is going to continue to grow over the next several decades. They predict that by the year 2050, about 60 million people will live there!

ACTIVITY

TEST YOUR KNOWLEDGE

It's time to take a little test! Don't worry—the quiz below will be fun. It will also help you learn a bit more about the history of the Colorado River. On the left side, you'll see the names of five people who are linked to the waterway. On the right side, you'll see the reasons these people earned their fame. Try to match each person with the correct description!

1) Francisco de Ulloa

A) U.S. explorer famous for mapping the Colorado River and for making the first successful journey on it through the Grand Canyon

2) Brigham Young

B) Spanish explorer who was probably the first European to come into contact with the Colorado River

3) Geronimo

C) Scientist who was one of the first women to complete a water voyage through the Grand Canyon along the Colorado River

4) John Wesley Powell

D) Leader of the Mormon faith who encouraged members of his church to set up some of the first permanent white settlements within the Colorado River's watershed

5) Elzada Clover

E) Apache leader who led raids against U.S. settlers throughout the Southwest, including portions of the Colorado River basin

Answers: 1) B; 2) D; 3) E; 4) A; 5) C

STOP
Don't write in this book!

In addition, people living in seven U.S. states use the river for everything from **hydroelectric** power to drinking water. Major cities within the basin include Tucson and Phoenix in Arizona, and Las Vegas in Nevada. But Americans as far away as Los Angeles, California, depend on the Colorado River, too.

Now that you've arrived at the Colorado River, consider kicking off your journey with a little outdoor activity. You can enjoy hiking, biking, or horseback riding on trails near the river's source in Rocky Mountain National Park. You'll find this park in north-central Colorado. If you're truly on the wild side, you'll do some white-water rafting in the Grand Canyon in Arizona or the Black Canyon in Nevada.

The Colorado River provides hydroelectric power to large cities such as Las Vegas, Neveda.

→ The Lost City Museum features
reconstructed Pueblo homes.

Would you prefer to explore *Apatosaurus* footprints instead? Follow the Colorado River to Moab, Utah. This place is famous for its dinosaur fossil tracks. While you're in the area, be sure to check out the unique sandstone arches and red rock towers that are found there.

Are you interested in learning about how American Indians helped shape local culture? Stop by the Colorado River Indian Tribes Museum and Library in Parker, Arizona. Visitors there can view historical documents as well as Native American jewelry, baskets, and pottery. Try to leave some time in your schedule to stroll through the Lost City Museum in Overton, Nevada. This lower basin attraction features exhibits related to ancient Pueblo peoples.

It's easy to get wrapped up in touring the Colorado River. Don't forget to grab a bite to eat! Ancestral Pueblo bean soup, Navajo fry bread, and Hopi corn stew are tasty examples of traditional American Indian dishes. You can sample these during your adventure.

Southwestern foods such as chili con carne (chili with meat) and carne asada (thinly sliced, grilled beef) are also popular in the upper and lower basins. This cuisine blends the cooking styles of early Spanish settlers, Native Americans, cowboys, and Mexicans living near the river. Beans, rice, vegetables, meat, and cheese are often ingredients in Southwestern meals. So are thin, flat cornmeal pancakes called tortillas.

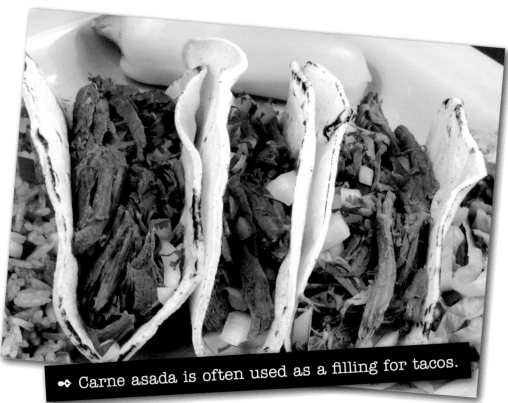

•◦ Carne asada is often used as a filling for tacos.

ACTIVITY RECIPE

A serving of Navajo fry bread is a surefire way to quiet your grumbling stomach as you explore the Colorado River. Fortunately, you don't need to be walking along the waterway to enjoy this delicious fried dough. Actually, you don't even need to fry Navajo fry bread! Baking it is much healthier. You can prepare baked Navajo fry bread at home using the simple recipe below. Be sure to have an adult help you operate your oven.

Baked Navajo Fry Bread

INGREDIENTS
1 cup white flour
1/4 teaspoon salt
1 teaspoon powdered milk
1 teaspoon baking powder
1/2 cup water

INSTRUCTIONS

1. Preheat your oven to 350°F (177°C).

2. Mix together all of the dry ingredients. Then add the water and continue stirring until a dough forms.

3. Find a clean surface, such as a countertop in your kitchen. Use your hands to knead, or shape, the dough into a ball.

4. Divide the dough into four parts. Flatten each piece with your hands or a rolling pin. Each piece should look like a pancake. (If your "pancakes" seem too sticky to work with, sprinkle a few pinches of flour on them.)

5. Once the oven is heated, lightly coat a baking pan with cooking spray. Place the four pieces of dough in the pan. Bake them for 10 minutes.

6. After the baked fry bread cools, share a slice of Colorado River cuisine with three of your friends! Since people often use fry bread like a taco shell, try filling each piece with chili, shredded lettuce, diced tomato, low-fat cheese, and sour cream.

CHAPTER FOUR

TAKING CARE OF A NATIONAL TREASURE

→ The Hoover Dam is one of the largest dams in the world.

Can you imagine the Colorado River running dry? This might sound silly, but it's no laughing matter. Growing numbers of people have moved into the watershed. They have cleared wetlands to build homes and businesses. They have also constructed canals and dams—including the famous Hoover Dam in Nevada—to redirect and control the flow of the river. Certain parts of the river actually do run dry as a result of this human activity.

ACTIVITY

GRAPHING THE COLORADO RIVER'S WATERSHED

Government officials have created agreements that divide water usage among the seven U.S. states in the Colorado River's watershed. For example, Colorado is assigned 24 percent of the river's water. New Mexico receives more than 5 percent and Utah gets 11 percent. Wyoming is allowed to use more than 6 percent. Meanwhile, Arizona has been granted about 17 percent of the Colorado River's water. California has almost 27 percent. Nevada can use nearly 2 percent. (The remaining water is used by Mexico.)

Review this information and create a bar graph illustrating water usage in the Colorado River basin in the United States. Can you guess which bar will be the longest? Which do you predict will be the shortest?

The good news is that Americans just like you can join in **conservation** efforts to save the Colorado River! Everyone from government officials to scientists to average kids can play a part in protecting the waterway. For starters, many U.S. citizens are paying closer attention to how they use water and are trying to avoid wasting it. People are also beginning to redirect the flow of the Colorado River to natural areas, instead of only farms and cities.

What can *you* do to look after the Lifeline of the Southwest? Educate the public! Talk to your friends, teachers, parents, and community leaders about your experiences along the Colorado River. Discuss the incredible wildlife you've studied, as well as the waterway's history, culture, and economy. Help spread the word about why the Colorado River is truly a national treasure. It must survive for centuries to come.

•◦ Can you think of a few other ways to help protect the Colorado River?

ACTIVITY

WRITE A LETTER

THE COLORADO RIVER

Government officials in Wyoming, Colorado, Utah, Arizona, New Mexico, Nevada, and Arizona are helping shape the future of the Colorado River. Along with other politicians across the rest of America, they vote on laws and organize projects that impact U.S. waterways. Writing a letter to these men and women lets them know that people like you care about the Colorado River. Ask an adult to help you find the addresses of officials who encourage conservation efforts in and along the river. Then create a short, simple letter using the following outline:

Dear [INSERT THE NAME OF THE POLITICIAN(S) YOU DECIDE TO WRITE TO]:

I am writing to ask for your help in protecting the Colorado River. The river is important to me because [INSERT TWO OR THREE REASONS THE RIVER MATTERS TO YOU]

Thanks for your efforts to support this amazing American waterway!

Sincerely,

[INSERT YOUR NAME]

STOP
Don't write in this book!

GLOSSARY

amphibians (am-FIB-ee-uhnz) cold-blooded animals with a backbone that live in water and breathe with gills when young; as adults, they develop lungs and live on land

backwaters (BAK-wah-tuhrz) parts of a river where there is no active flow

conservation (kahn-sur-VAY-shuhn) the protection of valuable things, especially wildlife, natural resources, forests, or artistic or historic objects

cuisine (kwi-ZEEN) a style of cooking or presenting food

economy (i-KAH-nuh-mee) the system of buying, selling, making things, and managing money in a place

ecosystem (EE-koh-sis-tuhm) all the livings things in a place and their relation to the environment

habitats (HAB-uh-tats) places where an animal or a plant usually lives

hydroelectric (hye-droh-i-LEK-trik) using the power of water to produce electricity

irrigate (IR-uh-gate) to supply water to crops by artificial means, such as channels or pipes

recreational (rek-ree-AY-shuhn-uhl) involving games, sports, and hobbies that people like to do in their spare time

springs (SPRINGZ) places where water rises to the surface from an underground source

tributaries (TRIB-yu-ter-eez) streams that flow into a larger stream, river, or lake

white-water (WYTE-WAH-tuhr) describing rapids or other portions of a river where the water is shallow and quick-moving

BOOKS

Lomberg, Michelle. *The Grand Canyon*. New York: AV2 by Weigl, 2013.

Rau, Dana Meachen. *The Southwest*. New York: Children's Press, 2012.

WEB SITES

DisneyFamily.com—Colorado River Rafting Maze
http://family.go.com/travel/vacations/arizona/grand-canyon /best-grand-canyon-vacation-282102-printable-424067
This Web site includes a printable maze that lets you pretend you're traveling through the Grand Canyon on the Colorado River.

Water Education Foundation—Colorado River Facts
www.watereducation.org/doc.asp?id=1025
This site features fast facts about the river, as well as an overview of conservation efforts.

INDEX

ABOUT THE AUTHOR
Katie Marsico has written more than 100 books for young readers. She isn't adventurous enough to try white-water rafting but would still like to see the Colorado River one day. Ms. Marsico dedicates this book to Pete, Alison, Hayden, Eme, and Finley Dondlinger.